And here's what you do!

1 Copy each step-by-step drawing onto your grid paper, noticing where the drawing should touch the lines on your grid. Draw lightly in pencil. Since each new step is shown in blue, you'll always know exactly what to do next.

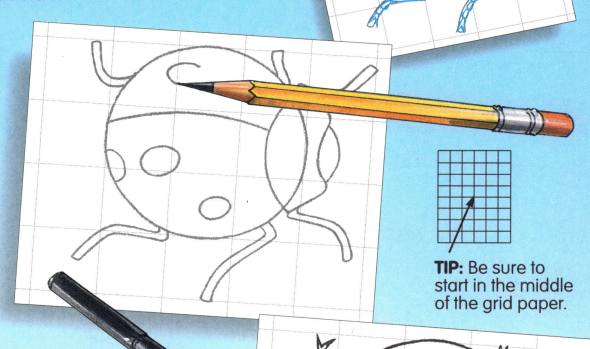

TIP: Be sure to start in the middle of the grid paper.

2 You may erase the pencil construction lines as you go along so that you can see how your drawing is progressing. When you have finished, use your felt-tip pen to go over the lines you want to keep, and erase any stray pencil lines.

Now you have a perfect drawing to color any way you'd like! Before you color, you may want to read pages 30 to 32 for some extra coloring tips.

3

Ladybug

Draw a circle for the shell and add a head and six legs. Divide the shell with a curved line.

1

Add spots, antennae, and details on the legs.

2

3

Use your felt-tip pen to trace over the lines you want to keep, and erase any stray pencil lines.

4 Color your ladybug!

4

Centipede

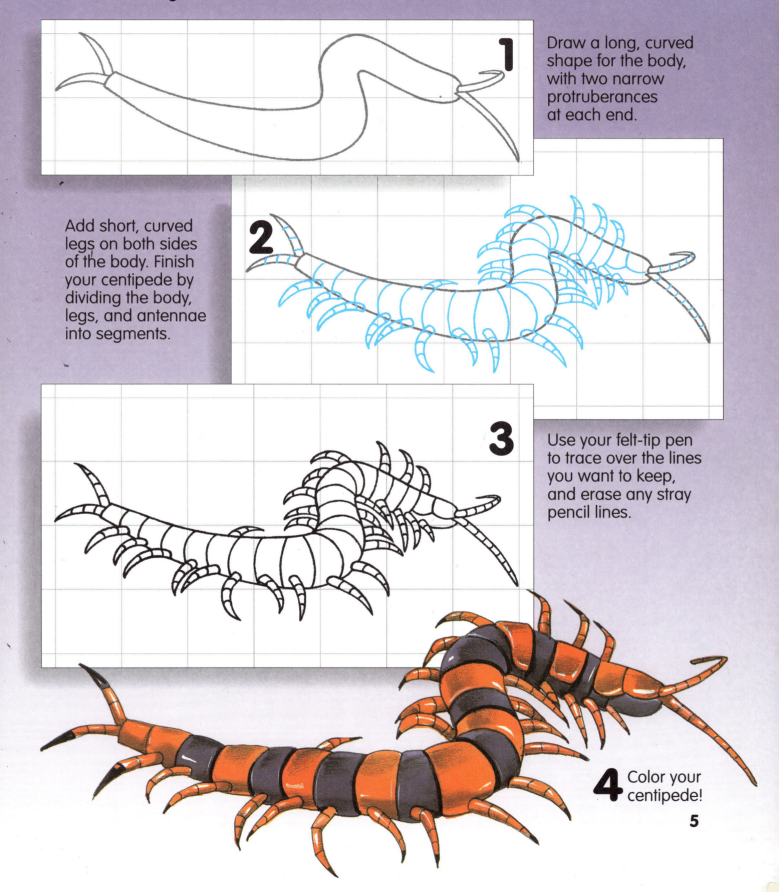

1 Draw a long, curved shape for the body, with two narrow protruberances at each end.

Add short, curved legs on both sides of the body. Finish your centipede by dividing the body, legs, and antennae into segments.

2

3

Use your felt-tip pen to trace over the lines you want to keep, and erase any stray pencil lines.

4 Color your centipede!

5

Stick Insect

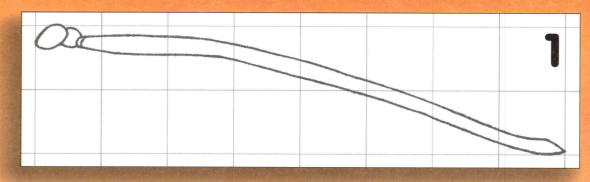

1

Draw a long, tubular body and a tiny head.

Add antennae, an eye, and body segments. Draw three small circles for leg joints, and add detail to the end of the body.

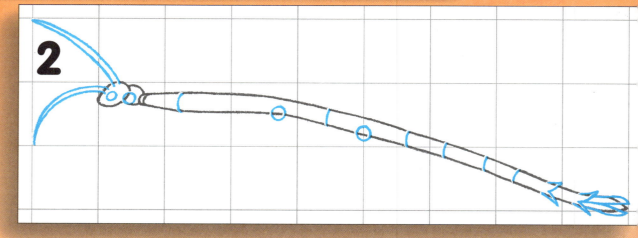

2

Draw two long, bent legs near the head and four more legs at the center of the body.

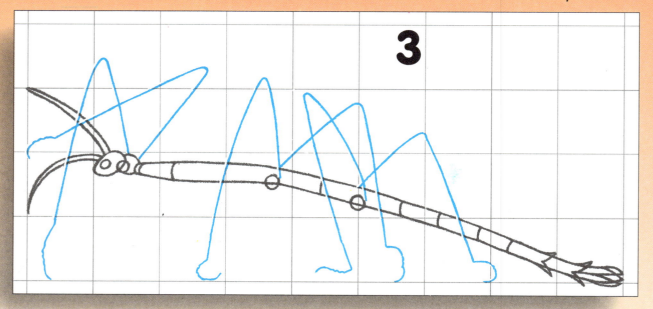

3

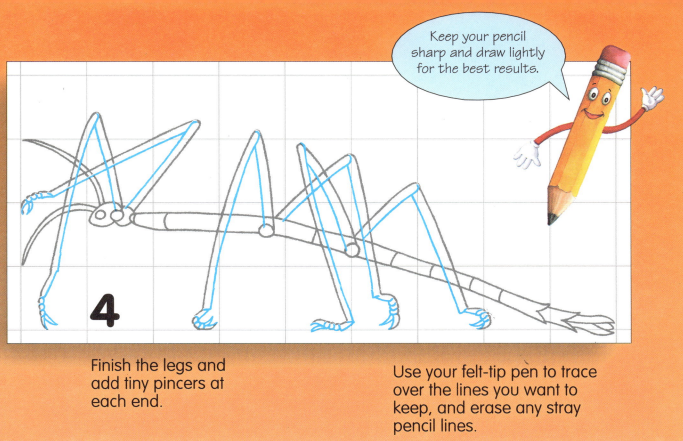

Keep your pencil sharp and draw lightly for the best results.

4

Finish the legs and add tiny pincers at each end.

Use your felt-tip pen to trace over the lines you want to keep, and erase any stray pencil lines.

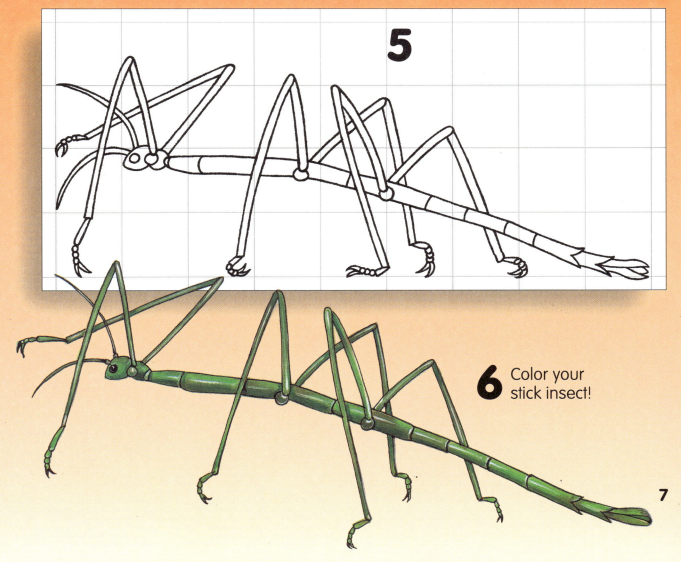

5

6 Color your stick insect!

Butterfly

Draw a circle for the head and a narrow, tapering abdomen.

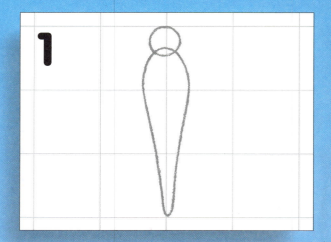

Add four large wings on each side of the abdomen. Draw spots on each wing.

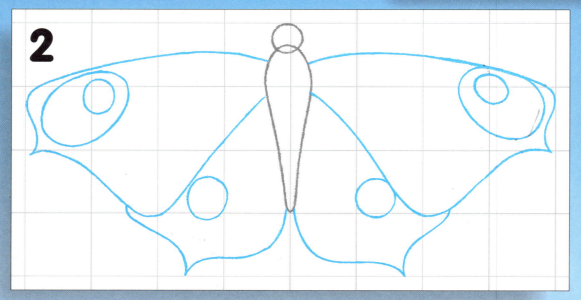

Detail the face with eyes and a mouth, or mandible. Draw the back and add more details to the wings.

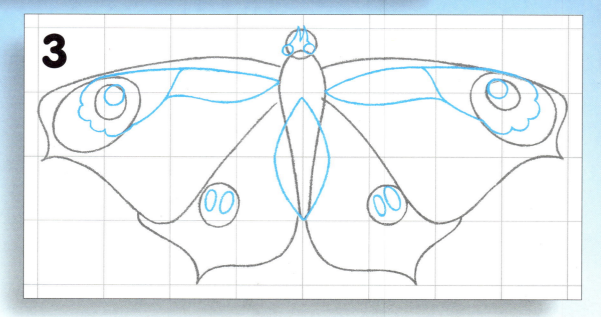

8

4 Give your butterfly antennae, segments on the body, and further details on the head and wings.

Use your felt-tip pen to trace over the lines you want to keep, and erase any stray pencil lines.

5

Butterflies come in just about every color, so let your imagination go wild!

6 Color your butterfly!

Bugs in Action

Bugs can hop, fly, creep, or scurry. You can make your bug move by keeping the body in one position and moving the position of the legs and wings. Since bugs don't usually travel in a straight line, your drawing will look even more realistic if you angle your bug and try showing it from different perspectives.

This butterfly's wings gently flutter down and then are brought together to show the stages of its flight. Learn to draw the butterfly on page 8.

The cricket launches into a hop by thrusting its body forward and straightening its powerful hind legs. Learn to draw the cricket on page 20.

Praying Mantis

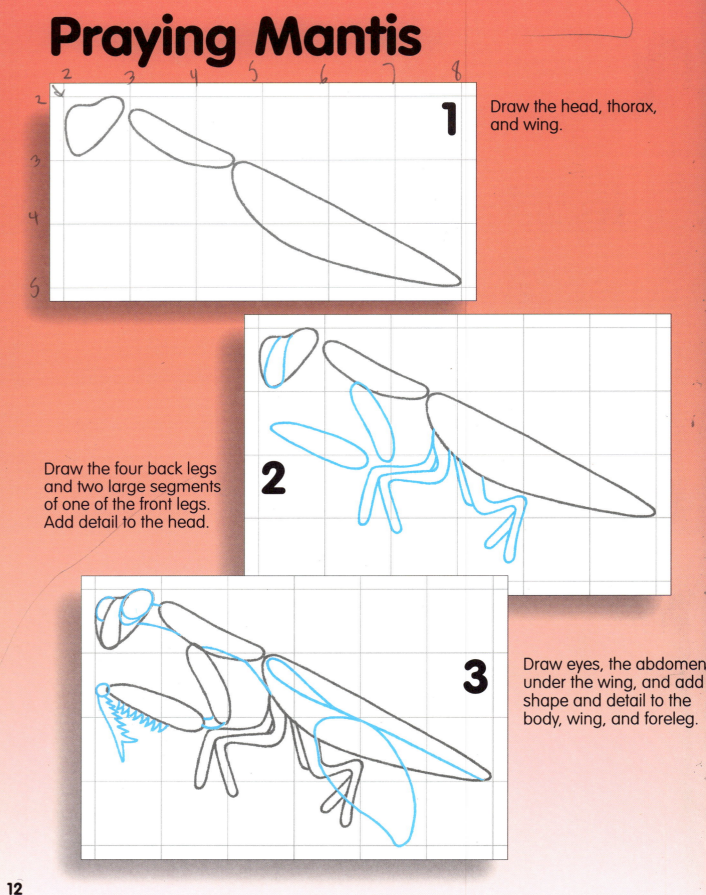

1 Draw the head, thorax, and wing.

2 Draw the four back legs and two large segments of one of the front legs. Add detail to the head.

3 Draw eyes, the abdomen under the wing, and add shape and detail to the body, wing, and foreleg.

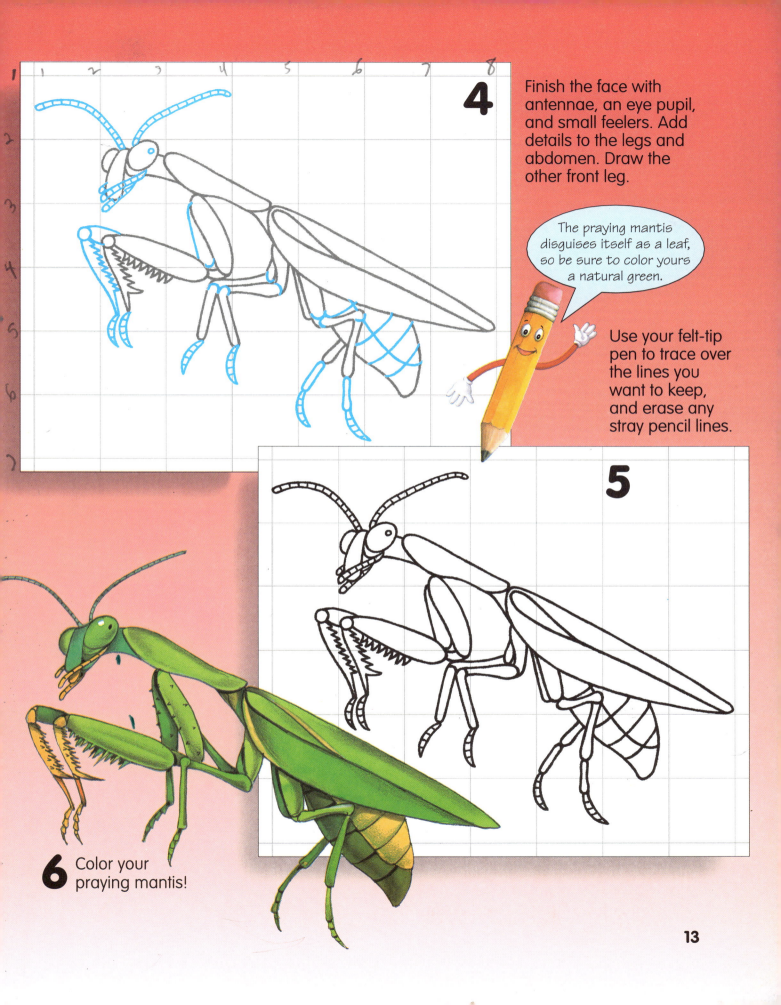

4 Finish the face with antennae, an eye pupil, and small feelers. Add details to the legs and abdomen. Draw the other front leg.

The praying mantis disguises itself as a leaf, so be sure to color yours a natural green.

Use your felt-tip pen to trace over the lines you want to keep, and erase any stray pencil lines.

5

6 Color your praying mantis!

Hercules Beetle

1

Draw an oval for the abdomen and a long curved shape for the top horn and head.

2

Draw the lower horn and the top segments of the legs. Add the underside of the abdomen.

3

Draw an eye and add the lower parts of the legs. Shape the horn.

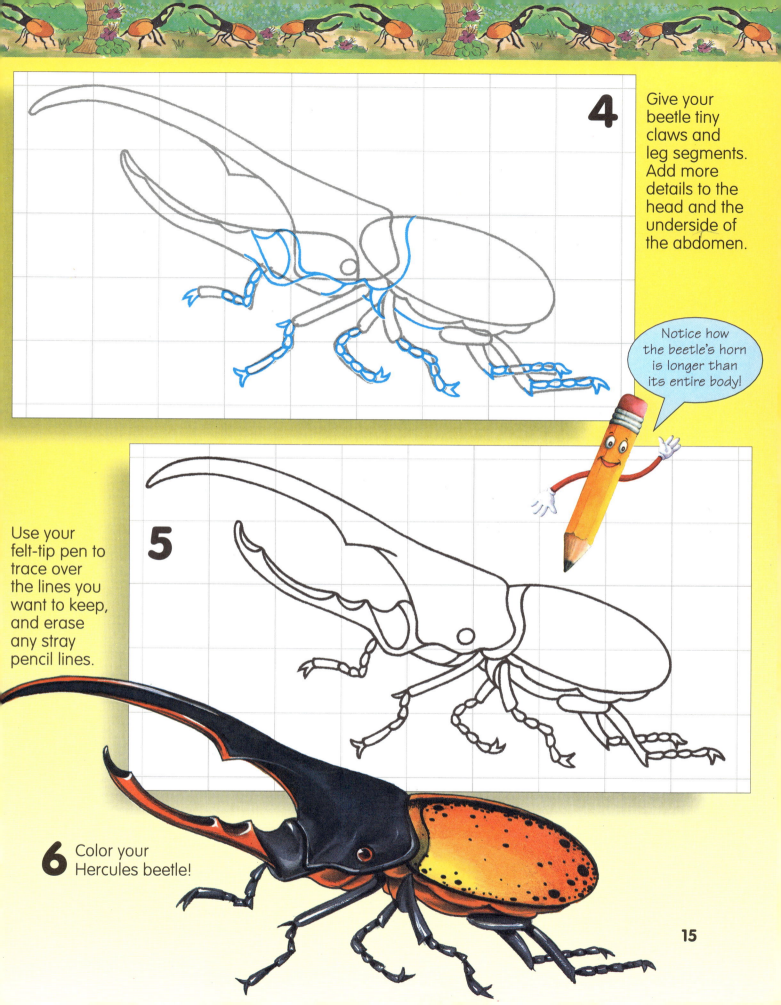

4 Give your beetle tiny claws and leg segments. Add more details to the head and the underside of the abdomen.

Notice how the beetle's horn is longer than its entire body!

5 Use your felt-tip pen to trace over the lines you want to keep, and erase any stray pencil lines.

6 Color your Hercules beetle!

Making Backgrounds

Bugs live in almost every part of the world, so it's only natural to show them in their respective habitats. Try copying the backgrounds shown here, and then explore your own surroundings for ideas on other bug homes!

Learn to draw the scorpion on page 22. ▲

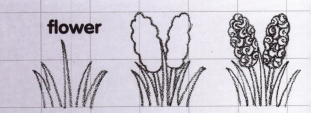

▲ Learn to draw the ladybug on page 4.

cactus

16

flower

▼ Learn to draw the butterfly on page 8.

Learn to draw the bee on page 26. ▲

▼ Learn to draw the cricket on page 20.

leaf

tree

17

Tarantula

1 Use simple circular and curved shapes to draw the tarantula's head, thorax, and abdomen.

2 Add the top segments of the visible legs, and a curved line to define the head.

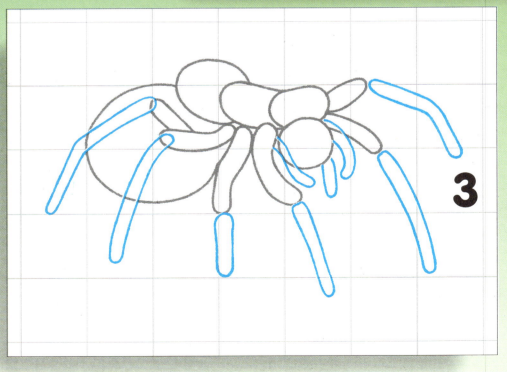

3 Draw the lower segments of the legs, and short feelers on the head.

4 Draw the eyes and mandible, and finish the legs.

When drawing bugs, it's a good idea to erase construction lines as you go along.

5 Use your felt-tip pen to trace over the lines you want to keep, and erase any stray pencil lines.

6 Color your tarantula!

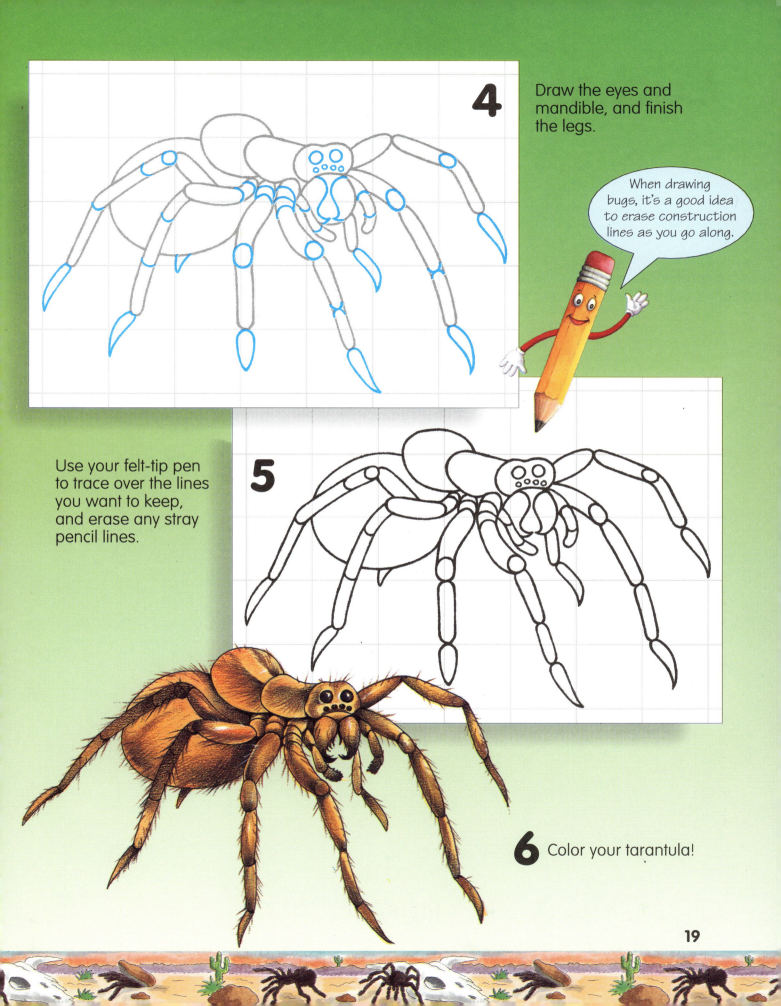

Cricket

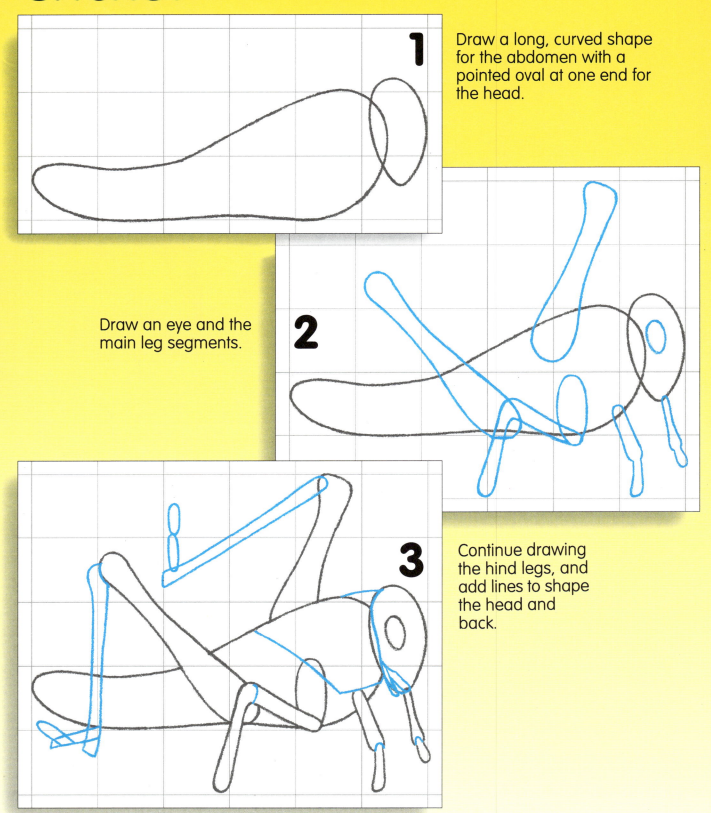

1 Draw a long, curved shape for the abdomen with a pointed oval at one end for the head.

Draw an eye and the main leg segments.

2

3 Continue drawing the hind legs, and add lines to shape the head and back.

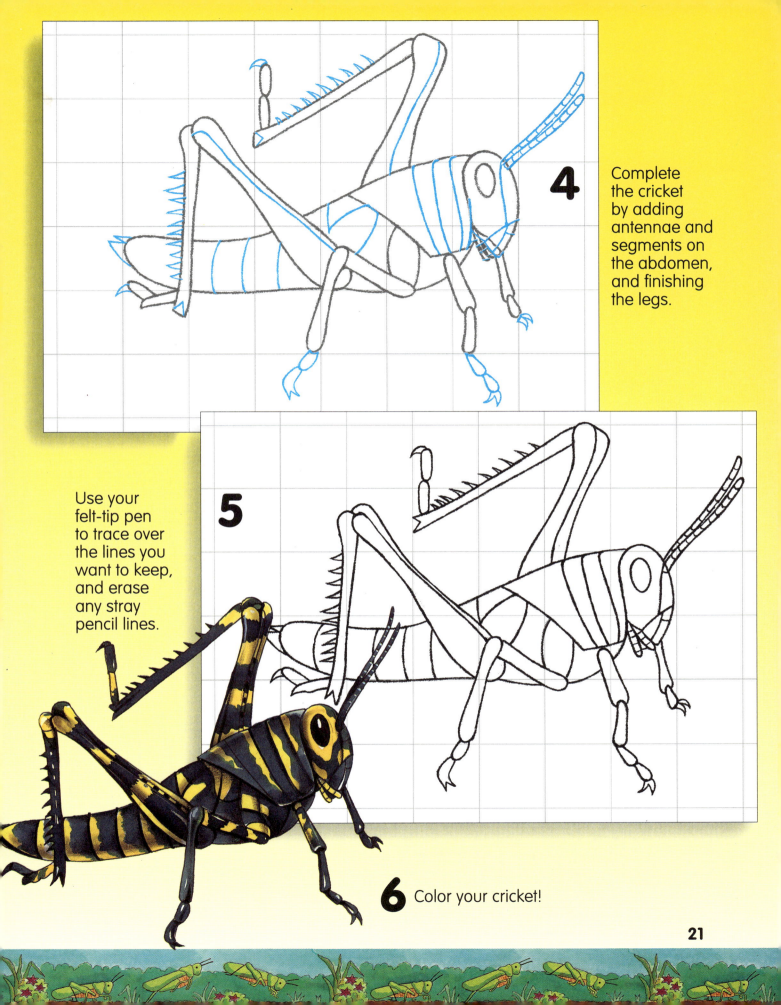

4 Complete the cricket by adding antennae and segments on the abdomen, and finishing the legs.

5 Use your felt-tip pen to trace over the lines you want to keep, and erase any stray pencil lines.

6 Color your cricket!

Scorpion

Draw the scorpion's body and front claws.

Use ovals and circles to make the scorpion's tail. Add the pincers and the sharp stinger at the end of the tail.

Add four legs on each side of the body.

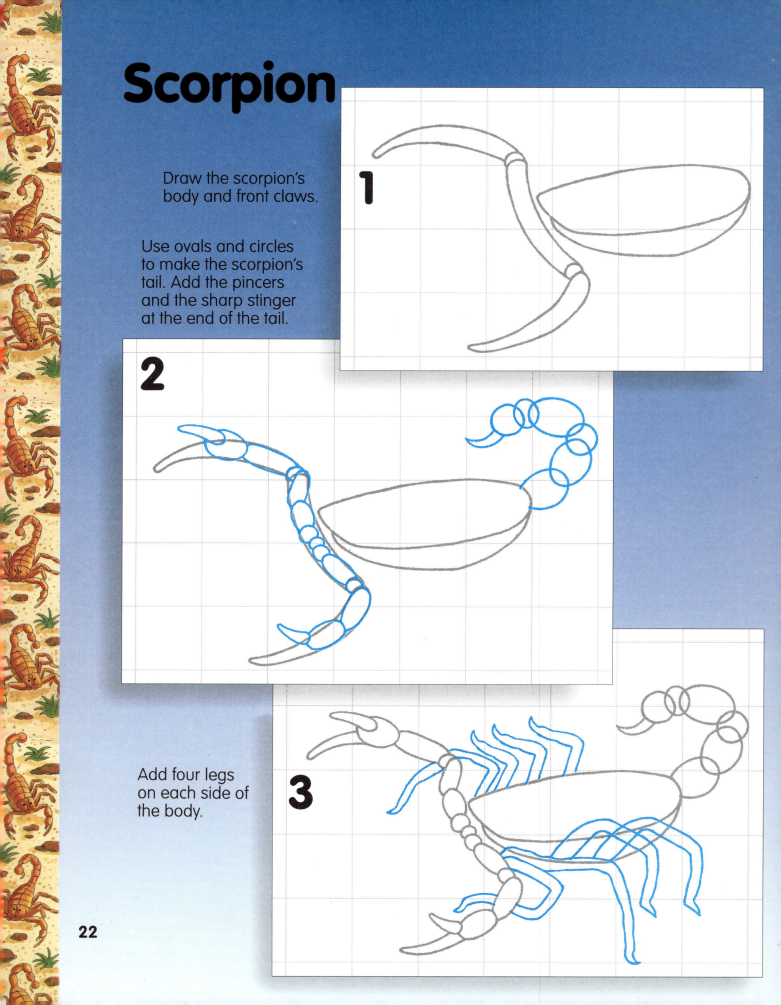

Use curved lines to divide the body and legs into segments. Add eyes and further details to the top of the head.

Use your felt-tip pen to trace over the lines you want to keep, and erase any stray pencil lines.

4

5

6 Color your scorpion!

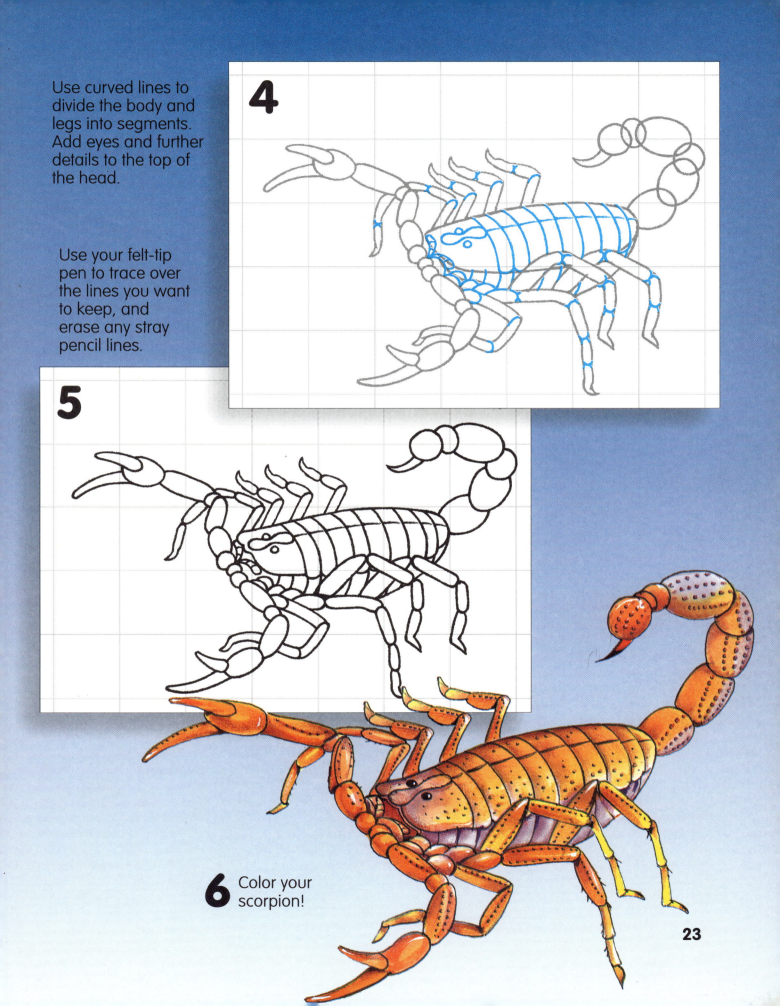

cloud

Putting It All Together

You can find a wide variety of bugs living in the same surroundings. Here is a scene showing some of the types of bugs you might find in a flower garden. A different scene might show the scorpion and tarantula in the desert. Remember that some bugs, such as the praying mantis, like to hide among leaves. The more you learn about bugs, the more realistic your drawing will be.

flower

grass

Bee

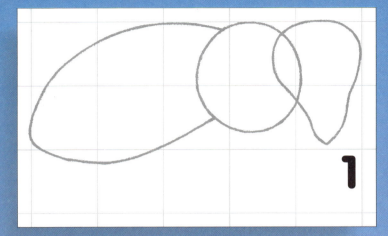

1 Draw a circle for the thorax, and add a long abdomen on one side and a pear-shaped head on the other.

Add the five visible legs, antennae segments, and details on the head and mandible.

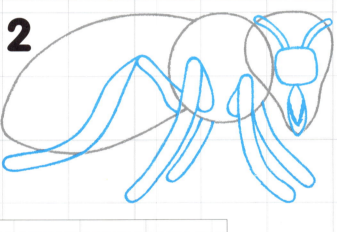

2

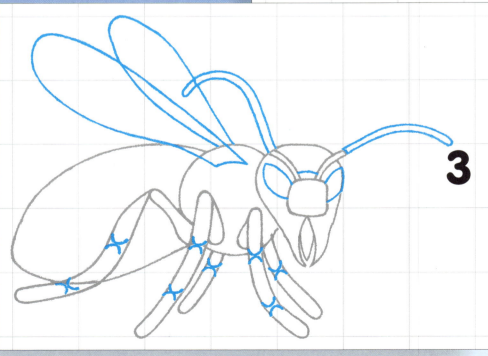

3 Finish the antennae and draw two long curved wings. Give your bee large eyes and divide the legs into segments.

4 Add stripes on the abdomen, four small feelers, and details on the legs and head to complete your drawing.

Use your felt-tip pen to trace over the lines you want to keep, and erase any stray pencil lines.

5

6 Color your bee!

Ant

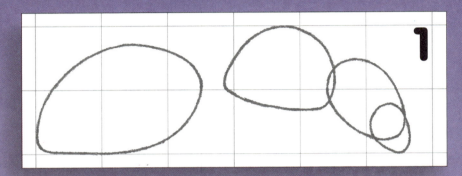

Draw three curved shapes for the ant's head, thorax, and abdomen. Add a small, overlapping oval on the head for the ant's mandible.

Add an eye, back leg segments, and details on the thorax.

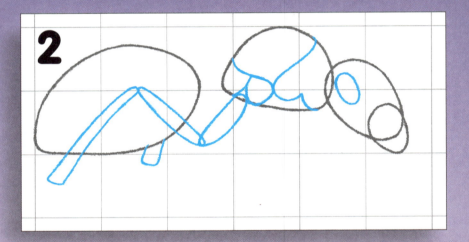

Draw more leg segments and define the mandible.

Finish your ant with antennae, the remaining leg segments, and curved lines on the abdomen. Connect the thorax to the abdomen with a narrow waist.

Use your felt-tip pen to trace over the lines you want to keep, and erase any stray pencil lines.

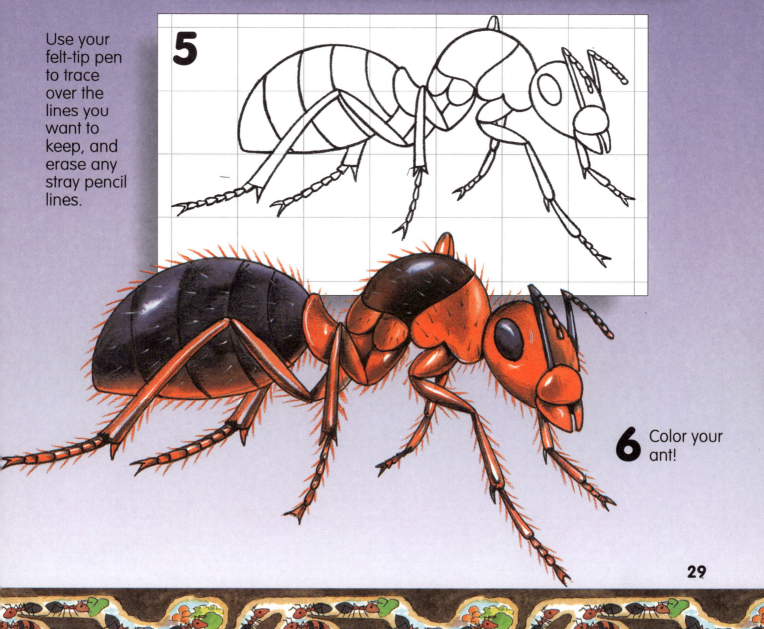

6 Color your ant!

Coloring Your Drawings

Once you've finished the outlines of your drawings, it's fun to color them in. Use watercolor paints, colored pencils, crayons, markers, or anything else you can think of!

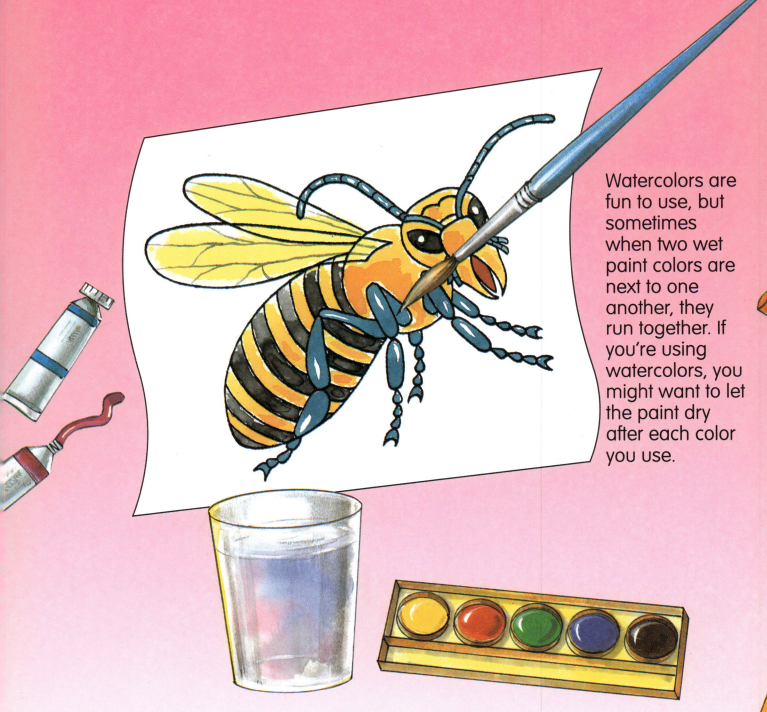

Watercolors are fun to use, but sometimes when two wet paint colors are next to one another, they run together. If you're using watercolors, you might want to let the paint dry after each color you use.

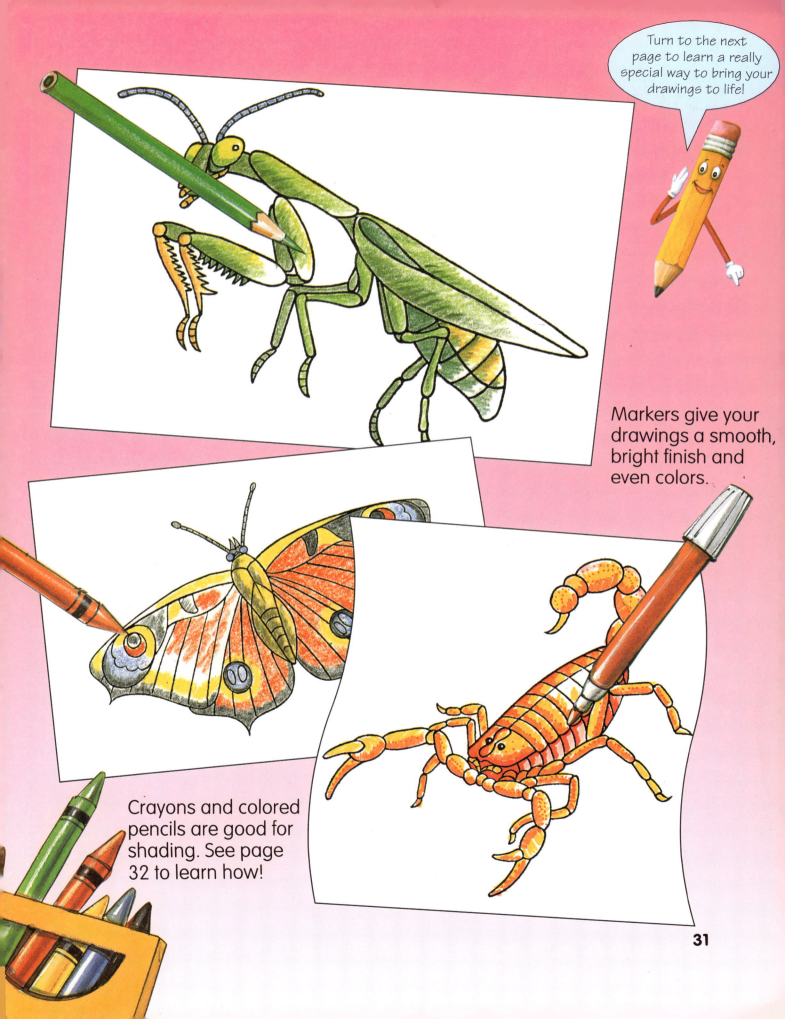

Turn to the next page to learn a really special way to bring your drawings to life!

Markers give your drawings a smooth, bright finish and even colors.

Crayons and colored pencils are good for shading. See page 32 to learn how!

31

Shading Your Drawings

Shading can add dimension and life to your drawings. When coloring your bugs, leave some areas lighter than others to show where the light would shine. Then try shading with a crayon, pencil, or colored pencil and watch your drawing come to life!

Use these pull-out grid pages for your drawings. Make extra copies so you can draw lots of pictures using the steps in this book!